Everyone is different,
No one's quite the same.
This book is all about YOU.
What is your name?

For Katie, Alice and Bridie

PUFFIN BOOKS
Published by the Penguin Group
Penguin USA, 375 Hudson Street, New York, New York 10014, U.S.A.
Penguin Books Ltd, 27 Wrights Lane, London W8 5TZ, England
Penguin Books Australia Ltd, Ringwood, Victoria, Australia
Penguin Books Canada Ltd, 10 Alcorn Avenue, Toronto, Ontario, Canada M4V 3B2
Penguin Books (N.Z.) Ltd, 182-190 Wairau Road, Auckland 10, New Zealand

Penguin Books Ltd, Registered Offices: Harmondsworth, Middlesex, England

First published in Great Britain by William Heinemann Ltd., 1991
First published in the United States of America by Viking,
a division of Penguin USA, 1992
Published in Puffin Books, 1994

1   3   5   7   9   10   8   6   4   2

Produced by Mandarin
Printed and bound in Hong Kong

Catherine and Laurence Anholt

ALL
ABOUT
YOU

PUFFIN BOOKS

When you wake up in the morning, how do you feel?

happy

tired

sad

noisy

quiet

glad

How do you feel today?

When you put on your clothes,

what do you wear?

shoes   shorts   shirt

jeans   sweater   skirt

jacket   underpants   vest

hat   scarf   dress

sandals   socks   suits

T-shirt   tights   boots

What are you wearing now?

When you look out your window, what do you see?

fields

town

sea

city

park   trees

What's outside?

Do you live in a brick house,

or something different?

town house   castle   barn

houseboat   igloo   farm

apartment   cottage   greenhouse

trailer   tent   tree house

What's your house like?

Does someone else live with you?

sister   granny   brother

father   baby   mother

Are you feeling hungry?
What do you like?

 carrots

 cabbage

 cheese

 pears

 pasta

 peas

 hot dogs

 honey

 ham

 juice

 Jell-O

jam

cake

curry

custard

melon

milk

mustard

pancakes

plums

potato

cornflakes

cupcake

cocoa

What's your favorite food?

Do you play with your friends?

jump

skip

chase

trip

fight

race

dance   climb   slide

run   leap   hide

What do you like to play?

Or do you play on your own?

What do you play with?

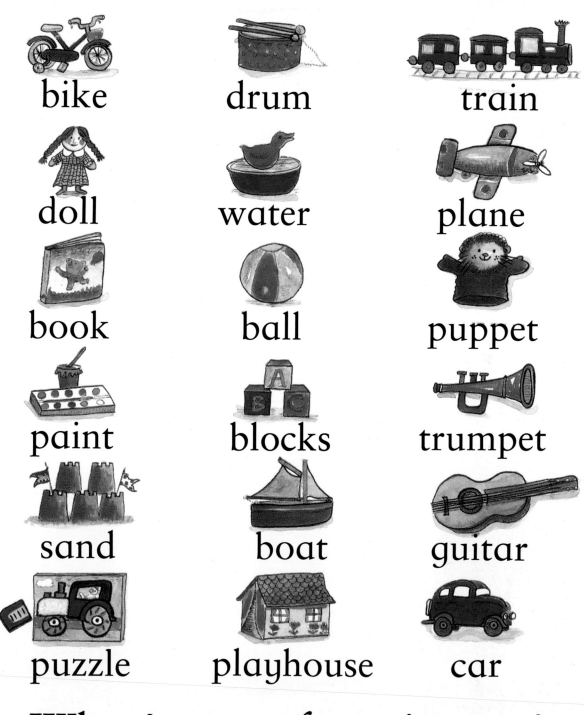

bike

drum

train

doll

water

plane

book

ball

puppet

paint

blocks

trumpet

sand

boat

guitar

puzzle

playhouse

car

What's your favorite toy?

Where do you like to go?

party

picnic

pool

zoo

library

school

Which do you like best?

Do you have a
special friend?

Or a pet?

What's your favorite animal?

bird

bear

bat

camel

cow

cat

walrus

wolf

whale

sheep

seal

snail

fish

fox

frog

donkey

duck

dog

monkey

mole

moose

gorilla

goat

goose

When it's time for bed, what do you do?

wash

dry

brush

dress

clean up

rush

Everyone is different,
No one's quite alike.
This book was all about you.
Now it's time to say...

GOOD NIGHT.